GW00683386

# SHENFIELD
# TO
# IPSWICH

Vic Mitchell

MP Middleton Press

*Front cover: Class B1 4-6-0 no. 61282 speeds through Witham on 6th October 1951 with a Cromer to Liverpool Street express. The maltings are in the background and part of the signal box is on the left. (B.W.L.Brooksbank)*

*Back cover upper: The new maltings at Witham can be seen above the DMU and a section of the later signal box is evident in front of it. The unit is working the 11.00 Lowestoft to Liverpool Street on 25th May 2005. (D.Pollock)*

*Back cover lower: The other end of Witham station is seen on 23rd March 2003, as no. 321362 calls forming the 12.25 Clacton to Liverpool Street service. The ticket office is top left; it was originally on the right. (T.Heavyside)*

*Published May 2011*

*ISBN 978 1 906008 96 3*

*© Middleton Press, 2011*

*Design Deborah Esher*

*Published by*
> *Middleton Press*
> *Easebourne Lane*
> *Midhurst*
> *West Sussex*
> *GU29 9AZ*

*Tel: 01730 813169*
*Fax: 01730 812601*
*Email: info@middletonpress.co.uk*
*www.middletonpress.co.uk*

*Printed in the United Kingdom by Henry Ling Limited, at the Dorset Press, Dorchester, DT1 1HD*

# INDEX

# ACKNOWLEDGEMENTS

I am very grateful for the assistance received from many of those mentioned in the credits also to P.G.Barnes, A.R.Carder, G.Croughton, R.R.Clow, A.G.W.Garraway, A.Grimmett, J.B.Horne, S.C.Jenkins, N.Langridge, B.Lewis, C.Phillips, Mr D. and Dr S. Salter and, in particular, my wife who has meticulously typeset my scribblings for almost 30 years.

I. Railway Clearing House map from about 1930.

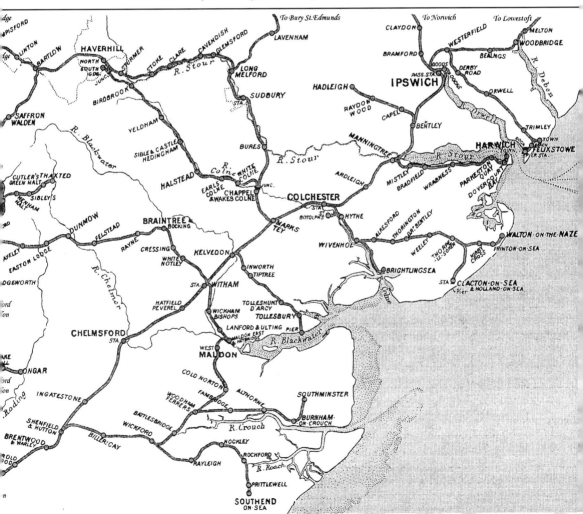

# GEOGRAPHICAL SETTING

Our journey starts on the outer limits of the almost continuous residential development around London. We soon pass over the small valley of the River Wid, which then runs roughly parallel to the route to Chelmsford, where it joins the River Can west of the town. This flows into the River Chelmer and we pass over this east of the county town.

The River Ter is crossed west of Hatfield Peverel and the River Brain at Witham. From here to Kelvedon, the route is close to the River Blackwater, which is bridged near to the station. Roman River is a minor watercourse and is traversed east of Marks Tey. The more significant River Colne is encountered on the approach to Colchester. It was notable in the development of this important Roman city, wharves being built on its west bank. The place developed as a busy commercial centre and has for long housed an Army garrison. It was famed for a destructive earthquake in 1884.

Shortly after leaving Manningtree, we pass from Essex into Suffolk as we cross over the first of two bridges over the River Stour. This widens and allowed docks to develop at Harwich and Felixstowe. Here it is joined by the River Orwell from Ipswich, where docks also grew to benefit the town.

The maps are to the scale of 25ins to 1 mile, with north at the top unless otherwise indicated.

Gradient profile with mileage from London.

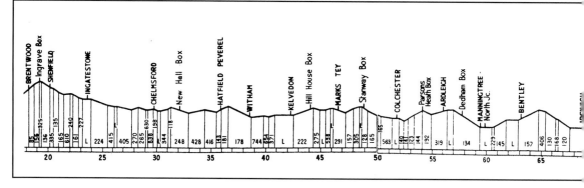

L. N. E. R.
**SERVICE, MILITARY, Etc.**
Not transferable. This ticket is issued subject to the notices & conditions in the Company's current time tables. AVAILABLE ON DAY OF ISSUE ONLY
COLCHESTER to
**LIVERPOOL ST**
Fare / S. M. Etc. / s. d.
No.......
THIRD / Colchester L'pool St \CLASS

Eastern Counties Railway.

**UP.**

CHELMSFORD to LONDON.

No. 1661 | s. | d.

1st Class - Paid | 7 | 0

# HISTORICAL BACKGROUND

The Eastern Counties Railway opened in stages from London and was completed to Brentwood in 1840. It was extended from there to Colchester on 29th March 1843 and was 5ft gauge throughout. The route was changed to standard gauge in 1844 and a line to Hythe Wharf from Colchester was opened for freight on 1st April 1847 by the Eastern Union Railway. It had opened the route from Colchester to Ipswich on 15th June 1846. Its trains ran north to Haughley later that year.

The aggressive disputes between these two companies will be passed over. However, they became constituents of the Great Eastern Railway in 1862.

From west to east, branches opened to passengers thus: Wickford and Southend (1888-89), Braintree and Maldon (1848), Tollesbury (1904), Sudbury (1849), Wivenhoe (1863 also to Brightlingsea and on to Walton and Clacton later), Harwich (1854) and Hadleigh (1847). Only three have closed and their closure dates, along with goods services, are given in the captions.

The GER became part of the London & North Eastern Railway in 1923 and this formed much of the Eastern Region of British Railways upon nationalisation in 1948.

The lines became part of Network SouthEast on 10th June 1986. Privatisation resulted in the routes being branded First Great Eastern on 5th January 1997 when FirstBus was awarded a 7¼ year franchise. This became First Group, but the operation was transferred to National Express, which applied the meaningless name of 'one' from 1st April 2004. It was rebranded National Express East Anglia in 2008.

## Electrification

Electric services at 1500 volts DC began between London and Shenfield in September 1949 and were extended to Chelmsford on 11th June 1956 and Southend Victoria on 31st December 1956. The change to 6250 volts AC took place in November 1960 and it was increased to 25kV by March 1961 to Chelmsford, after clearances had been increased.

The Colchester to Clacton and Walton section was electrified separately, a partial service starting on 16th March 1959. The gap between Chelmsford and Colchester saw some electric trains from 18th June 1962, with the full service starting 12 months later.

Colchester - Ipswich followed on 13th May 1985, Manningtree - Harwich Town on 12th May 1986 and Ipswich - Norwich on 11th May 1987.

The wiring to Ipswich had been completed in October 1983, as had Stratford to Willesden. This allowed container traffic to be hauled by class 86 electrics; passengers had to wait for this joy.

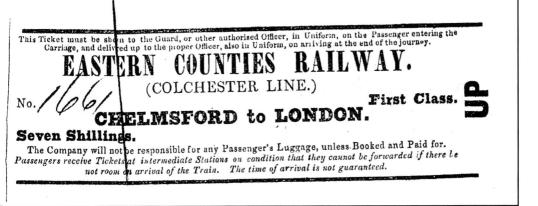

This Ticket must be shewn to the Guard, or other authorised Officer, in Uniform, on the Passenger entering the Carriage, and delivered up to the proper Officer, also in Uniform, on arriving at the end of the journey.

**EASTERN COUNTIES RAILWAY.**

(COLCHESTER LINE.)

First Class. UP

No. *1661*

**CHELMSFORD to LONDON.**

**Seven Shillings.**

The Company will not be responsible for any Passenger's Luggage, unless Booked and Paid for. *Passengers receive Tickets at intermediate Stations on condition that they cannot be forwarded if there be not room on arrival of the Train. The time of arrival is not guaranteed.*

# PASSENGER SERVICES

The GER provided six weekday trains and four on Sundays (this day is shown in brackets hereon) from London to Colchester in the early years. The EUR also offered these numbers, but the connections were poor - see 1850 timetables. One Sunday train terminated at Chelmsford at that time.

Twenty years later, the numbers were the same, but the stopping pattern was different. In 1890, there were ten (3) trains running the full length of the route, with two as far as Colchester, one Harwich boat train and two terminating at Ingatestone.

By 1910, Colchester was receiving 26(8) and Ipswich 21(6) from London, there being many short workings by that time. The figures also exclude trains from the branches for short distances. The figures thereafter increased steadily, except during wartime.

The first electric service to Chelmsford comprised one train per hour. The period of local diesel working on the non-electrified section between Chelmsford and Colchester in 1959-61 brought an infrequent timetable with trains starting from the former at 7.50am, 12.25, 5.42pm and from Witham at 8.34, 9.34am and 1.12pm. Few of these ran at weekends, but some through trains stopped at intermediate stations.

From 1963, the basic weekday pattern of departures from Liverpool Street was thus: on the even hours - Clacton, calling at all stations on our route; on the even half hours - Norwich, calling at Shenfield and Colchester; on the odd hours - Clacton, not stopping at Hatfield Peverel, Kelvedon or Marks Tey; on the odd half hours - Norwich, fast to Colchester. There were fewer on Sundays. Several of the trains from the Sudbury branch ran through Colchester to terminate at St. Botolphs at that period. In recent times, most have finished at Marks Tey.

The advent of electric traction to Norwich in 1987 brought a new departure sequence from Liverpool Street: xx.10 Harwich Town, xx.30 Norwich, xx.40 Clacton and xx.44 Witham, on weekdays. There were two per hour on Sundays.

March 1850

**Norwich, Bury, Ipswich, Hadleigh, Colchester, and London.**—Eastern Union.
C. Cobbold, M.P., Chairman.—J. F. Saunders, Sec.—P. Bruff, Eng. & Manr.—J. H. Sollas, Goods Supt.

| Miles. | Down. For Stations between London and Colchester, page 32. | Week Days. | | | | | | Sundays. | | | |
|---|---|---|---|---|---|---|---|---|---|---|---|
| | | 1 2 3 class. | 1 2 3 gov. | 1 & 2 mail. | 1 & 2 class. | 1 & 2 class | 1 & 2 mail. | 1 2 3 gov. | 1 2 3 gov. | 1 2 3 gov. | 1 & 2 mail. |
| | | morn | morn | morn | aft. | aft. | aft. | morn | morn | aft. | aft. |
| — | **London** ......dep. | .. | 8 10 | 11 0 | 3 30 | 5 30 | 8 30 | .. | 8 0 | 6 0 | 8 30 |
| 51¼ | **Colchester** ...... | 7 30 | 10 50 | 1 10 | 5 35 | 8 5 | 10 49 | 7 30 | 10 55 | 8†40 | 10 49 |
| 55¼ | Ardleigh............ | .. | 11 2 | .. | 5 45 | 8 17 | 11 2 | .. | 11 7 | 8 51 | 11 2 |
| 59 | Manningtree........ | 7 50 | 11 13 | 1 25 | 5 55 | 8 28 | 11 15 | 7 50 | 11 19 | 9 2 | 11 15 |
| 62¼ | Bentley Junction .. | 8 0 | 11 25 | 1 38 | 6 8 | 8 40 | .. | 8 0 | 11 29 | 9 13 | .. |
| Hadleigh Branch 64¾ | Capel ......ad | 8 25 | 11 35 | 1 55 | 6 23 | .. | .. | .. | .. | .. | .. |
| Hadleigh Branch 67½ | Raydon ......ad | 8 35 | 11 43 | 2 3 | 6 30 | .. | .. | .. | .. | .. | .. |
| Hadleigh Branch 69¾ | **Hadleigh** arr | 8 45 | 11 52 | 2 10 | 6 40 | .. | .. | .. | .. | .. | .. |
| 68 | **Ipswich** ........ | 8 10 | 11 50 | 1 50 | 6 20 | 8 56 | 11 39 | 8 15 | 11 43 | 9 27 | 11 39 |
| 70¾ | Bramford .......... | 8 18 | 12 0 | .. | 6 30 | | | .. | | | |
| 73 | Claydon............ | .. | 12 10 | .. | 6 38 | .. | .. | .. | | | |
| 76¾ | Needham .......... | 8 28 | 12 20 | 2 10 | 6 47 | .. | .. | 8 28 | | | |
| 80 | Stowmarket........ | 8 36 | 12 30 | 2 20 | 6 56 | .. | .. | 8 36 | | | |
| 82½ | Haughley Junction.. | 8 45 | 12 45 | 2 30 | 7 5 | .. | .. | 8 45 | | | |
| Bury Branch 86 | Elmswell ...... | 8 58 | 12 55 | 2 40 | 7 15 | .. | .. | 8 58 | | | |
| Bury Branch 90½ | Thurston ...... | 9 10 | 1 5 | 2 50 | 7 25 | .. | .. | 9 10 | | | |
| Bury Branch 94½ | **Bury** .... arr. | 9 20 | 1 15 | 3 0 | 7 35 | .. | .. | 9 20 | | | |
| 86¼ | Finningham ...... | 9 0 | 12 55 | .. | 7 18 | .. | .. | 9 0 | | | |
| 91 | Mellis (Eye) ...... | 9 10 | 1 5 | 2 55 | 7 30 | .. | .. | 9 10 | | | |
| 94½ | **Diss** .......... | 9 20 | 1 15 | 3 5 | 7 40 | .. | .. | 9 20 | | | |
| 97 | **Burston** ........ | 9 30 | 1 23 | .. | 7 47 | .. | .. | 9 30 | | | |
| 100 | Tivetshall.......... | 9 39 | 1 32 | 3 10 | 7 56 | .. | .. | 9 39 | | | |
| 103½ | Forncett .......... | 9 48 | 1 42 | 3 25 | 8 5 | .. | .. | 9 48 | | | |
| 106 | Flordon............ | 9 55 | 1 50 | .. | 8 15 | .. | .. | 9 55 | | | |
| — | Swainsthorpe ...... | .. | .. | .. | .. | .. | .. | .. | | | |
| 113½ | **Norwich**........ | 10 20 | 2 10 | 3 50 | 8 30 | .. | .. | 10 20 | | | |

**Norwich** to Yarmouth and Lowestoft, page 27; to Ely and Peterbro', page 28 & 27; to Dereham and Fakenham, pages 28 & 27; to Cambridge, St. Ives, and Huntingdon, pages 26, 27, & 24.

**BURY BRANCH.**—From BURY to NORWICH, on Week Days, at 8 10 morn., 12¼, 1 50, and 6 20 aft.—From NORWICH to BURY, on Week Days, at 7 20 and 11½ morn., and 5½ aft.—FARES between Bury & Norwich, 1st cl. 9s. 5d.; 2d cl. 5s. 8d.; 3d cl. 3s. 10½d.

**HADLEIGH BRANCH.**—From NORWICH to HADLEIGH, on Week Days, at 7 20 & 11½ morn., 4¼ aft.—From HADLEIGH to NORWICH, on Week Days, at 11 morn., 1 17 & 5 40 aft.

## LONDON, STRATFORD & CHELMSFORD, to COLCHESTER & BURY.—Eastern Counties.

| Miles | Down. From Shoreditch Station. | Week Days. | | | | | | | | | Sundays. | | | | | Fares. | | | |
|---|---|---|---|---|---|---|---|---|---|---|---|---|---|---|---|---|---|---|---|
| | | 1 2 3 gov. | mail, 1 2cl. | 1 2 3 class. | 1 & 2 1 cl. | 1 2 3 qck. clss | 1 & 2 cls. | 1 2 3 cls. | 1 & 2 mail. | 1 & 2 class. | 1 2 3 gov. | 1 2 3 class. | 1 2 3 cls. | 1 2 cls. | 1 & 2 mail. | 1st cl. s. d. | 2d.cl. s. d. | 3 cls. s. d. | gov. s. d. |
| | | morn | morn | aft | aft. | aft | aft | aft | aft | aft. | mrn | morn | aft | aft | aft | | | | |
| — | LONDON ..dep. | 8 10 | 11 0 | 1 20 | 3 30 | 4 20 | 5 30 | 6 30 | 8 30 | 10 15 | 8 0 | 10 15 2 45 | 6 0 | 8 30 | | | | | |
| 1 | Mile End ...... | 8 13 | .. | 1 33 | .. | 4 23 | .. | .. | .. | .. | 8 3 | 10 18 2 48 | 6 3 | .. | | 0 4 | 0 3 | 0 2 | 0 1 |
| 2¼ | Victoria Prk & Bow | 8 17 | .. | 1 37 | .. | 4 27 | .. | 6 35 | .. | .. | 8 7 | 10 22 2 52 | 6 7 | .. | | 0 4 | 0 3 | 0 2 | 0 2 |
| 3½ | Stratford ...... | 8 25 | 11 10 | 1 45 | .. | 4 33 | 5 41 | 6 40 | 8 40 | 10 30 | 8 15 | 10 28 2 58 | 6 13 | 8 40 | | 0 6 | 0 4 | 0 3 | 0 3 |
| 5 | Forest Gate .... | 8 30 | .. | 1 50 | .. | 4 37 | 5 45 | 6 44 | .. | .. | 8 20 | 10 31 3 | 16 | 17 | | 1 0 | 0 8 | 0 5 | 0 5 |
| 7 | Ilford .......... | 8 38 | 11 17 | 1 58 | 3 46 | 4 44 | 5 52 | 6 51 | 8 49 | .. | 8 30 | 10 37 3 | 7 6 26 | 8 46 | | 1 4 | 1 0 | 0 7 | 0 7 |
| 12 | Romford ...... | 8 52 | 11 28 | 2 12 | 3 58 | 4 55 | 6 7 | 7 8 | 8 54 | .. | 8 46 | 10 52 3 22 | 6 39 | 8 54 | | 2 6 | 1 9 | 1 0 | 0 11 |
| 17½ | Brentwood ...... | 9 7 | 11 45 | 2 30 | 4 11 | 5 10 | 6 23 | 7 25 | 9 11 | .. | 9 6 | 10 53 4 06 | 55 | 9 11 | | 3 9 | 2 9 | 1 9 | 1 5¼ |
| 19½ | Shenfield ...... | 9 14 | .. | .. | .. | .. | .. | 7 32 | .. | .. | 9 13 | .. | 3 46 | 7 1 | .. | 4 3 | 3 3 | 2 0 | 1 7½ |
| 23¼ | Ingatestone .... | 9 23 | 11 56 | .. | 4 24 | .. | 6 40 | 7 42 | 9 35 | .. | 9 23 | .. | 3 55 | 7 12 | 9 35 | 5 3 | 4 0 | 2 6 | 1 11 |
| 29½ | Chelmsford.. | 9 40 | 12 10 | .. | 4 37 | .. | 6 55 | 7 53 | 9 48 | .. | 9 38 | .. | 4 30 | 7 27 | 9 48 | 6 9 | 5 3 | 3 4 | 2 5 |
| 38½ | Witham ...... | 10 5 | 12 30 | .. | 4 54 | .. | 7 22 | .. | 10 13 | .. | 10 4 | .. | .. | 7 51 | 10 13 | 9 0 | 6 9 | 5 3 | 3 2 |
| 41½ | Kelvedon ...... | 10 17 | 12 40 | .. | 5 1 | .. | 7 33 | .. | 10 23 | .. | 10 15 | .. | .. | 8 2 | 10 23 | 9 7 | 6 6 | 3 5 | 3½ |
| 46¼ | Marks Tey Jun.. | 10 30 | 12 50 | .. | 5 16 | .. | 7 44 | .. | .. | .. | 10 26 | .. | .. | 8 13 | .. | 11 0 | 8 9 | 6 3 | 3 10 |
| 51¼ | Colchester arr | 10 50 | 1 10 | .. | 5 35 | .. | 8 5 | .. | 10 49 | .. | 10 55 | .. | .. | 8 40 | 10 49 | 12 6 | 10 0 | 7 3 | 4 3 |
| 68 | Ipswich ...... | 11 50 | 1 50 | .. | 6 20 | .. | 8 56 | .. | 11 39 | .. | .. | .. | .. | .. | 11 39 | .. | .. | .. | .. |
| 94½ | Bury St.Edm. | 1 15 | 3 0 | .. | 7 35 | .. | .. | .. | .. | .. | .. | .. | .. | .. | .. | .. | .. | .. | .. |

| Miles | For stations between Bury and Colchester, p 33 | Week Days. | | | | | | | | Sundays. | | | | | Fares fm Colchester | | | |
|---|---|---|---|---|---|---|---|---|---|---|---|---|---|---|---|---|---|---|
| | | 1 & 2 mail | 1 2 3 cls. | 1 & 2 qck. | 1 2 3 clss. | 1 & 2 mail. | 1 & 2 cls. | 2 3 class. | 1 2 3 gov. | 1 & 2 mail | 1 2 3 morn | 3 1 2 class. | 1 2 3 class. | 1 2 3 cls. | 1st.cl. s. d. | 2d.cl. s. d. | 3 cl. s. d. | gov s. d. |
| | | mrn | mrn | mrn | morn | .. | aft. | aft. | aft. | mrn | morn | aft | aft | aft | | | | |
| — | Bury St.Ed ... | .. | .. | .. | .. | 8 10 | 12 15 | .. | 4 50 | .. | .. | .. | .. | .. | | | | |
| 26¼ | Ipswich ...... | 1 20 | .. | 7 0 | .. | 9 30 | 1 30 | .. | 6 0 | 1 20 | .. | .. | .. | .. | | | | |
| 43½ | Colchester ... | 2 11 | * | 7 45 | .. | 10 25 | 2 29 | .. | 6 45 | 2 11 | 9 30 | 5 15 | .. | .. | | | | |
| 48½ | Marks Tey .... | .. | .. | 7 56 | .. | 10 35 | 2 29 | .. | 7 3 | .. | 9 41 | 5 25 | .. | .. | 1 3 | 1 0 | 0 9 | 0 5 |
| 52¾ | Kelvedon ...... | 2 37 | .. | 8 9 | .. | 10 43 | 2 41 | .. | 7 15 | 2 37 | 9 52 | 5 38 | .. | .. | 2 3 | 1 6 | 1 0 | 0 9½ |
| 56¼ | Witham ...... | 2 47 | .. | 8 20 | .. | 11 7 | 2 51 | .. | 7 25 | 2 47 | 10 7 | 5 47 | p.m. | .. | 2 9 | 2 3 | 1 9 | 1 1 |
| 65½ | Chelmsfrd. | 3 12 | 7 40 | 8 45 | .. | 11 30 | 3 8 | .. | 7 50 | 3 12 | 10 32 | 6 11 | 8 0 | .. | 4 9 | 3 9 | 2 9 | 1 10 |
| 71½ | Ingatestone ... | 3 26 | 7 55 | 8 58 | .. | 11 45 | 3 25 | .. | 8 5 | 3 26 | 10 49 | 6 30 | 8 20 | .. | 7 0 | 5 0 | 3 9 | 2 4 |
| 74¾ | Shenfield .... | .. | 8 7 | 9 7 | .. | .. | .. | 8 14 | .. | .. | 11 2 | .. | 8 30 | .. | 7 9 | 6 0 | 4 3 | 2 6½ |
| 76¾ | Brentwood ... | 3 41 | 8 15 | 9 13 | 10 35 | 11 58 | 3 39 | 5 20 | 8 20 | 3 41 | 11 8 | 6 45 | 8 35 | 9 0 | 8 6 | 6 3 | 4 6 | 2 8½ |
| 82¼ | Romford ...... | 3 57 | 8 32 | 9 30 | 10 50 | 12 13 | 3 55 | 5 30 | 8 35 | 3 57 | 11 24 | 7 3 | 8 53 | 9 15 | 9 3 | 7 3 | 5 3 | 3 3 |
| 87½ | Ilford ........ | 4 12 | 8 43 | 9 43 | 11 4 | 12 27 | 4 8 | 5 40 | 8 49 | 4 12 | 11 39 | 7 16 | 9 8 | 9 29 | 11 0 | 8 6 | 5 3 | 3 8 |
| 89¼ | Forest Gate . | .. | 8 49 | .. | 11 12 | .. | 4 13 | 5 47 | 9 55 | .. | 11 47 | 7 22 | 9 14 | 9 37 | 11 9 | 9 0 | 6 9 | 3 10 |
| 90¾ | Stratford.. | 4 28 | 8 54 | 9 55 | 11 17 | 12 36 | 4 19 | 5 5 | 9 4 | 4 22 | 11 57 | 7 25 | 9 22 | 9 42 | 11 9 | 9 3 | 6 9 | 3 11¼ |
| 92 | Vic.Park&Bow | 9 0 | .. | 11 25 | .. | .. | 5 56 | 9 10 | .. | .. | .. | 9 32 | .. | 12 6 | 10 0 | 7 3 | 3 4 | |
| 93¼ | Mile End ..... | .. | 9 6 | .. | 11 29 Wed. | .. | 6 29 | 13 | .. | 12 8 | .. | 9 36 | 9 52 | 12 | 6 10 | 10 7 | 3 4 | 3 4 |
| 94½ | London .. arr | 4 30 | 9 10 | 11 35 | 12 50 | 4 35 | 6 15 | 9 20 | 4 30 | 12 15 | 7 40 | 9 45 | 10 0 | 12 | 6 10 | 10 7 | 3 4 | 3 4 |

+ 3rd class mail from Bury. ‡ 1 & 2 only from Bury.

* From Colchester on Mondays at 6 45 a.m. call-ing at all Stations except Mile End. 1st and 2nd class Day Tickets issued to London. The Black line lines under certain arrivals above that those trains run no further.

March 1850
December 1870

## LONDON, CHELMSFORD, COLCHESTER, HARWICH, IPSWICH, WOODBRIDGE, LOWESTOFT, YARMOUTH, & NORWICH.—G.E.

| Miles | For Fares see pages 84 and 85. | | | | | | | | | | | | | | | | | | | | | | | |
|---|---|---|---|---|---|---|---|---|---|---|---|---|---|---|---|---|---|---|---|---|---|---|---|---|
| — | Bishopsgate ...dep | | | 8 45 | | | 7 20 | 9 15 | 10 3 | 1110 | 1145 | 1215 | 1 0 | 2 30 | 3 | 5 3 | 3 | 4 55 | 5 39 | 6 30 | 7 | 1015 | 1020 | 10 30 |
| 2¾ | Mile End ...... | | | | | | 7 24 | | 10 6 | Wd | | 1218 | 3 | | | | | | 5 42 | | | | | 1020¾ | 1033 |
| 3¾ | Stratford ...... | | | 8 54 | | | 7 35 | 9 25 | 1015 | | 1120 | | 1227 | 1 12 | 2 39 | 3 17 | | | 5 49 | | | | | 1023½ | 1043 |
| 4¾ | Forest Gate ... | | | 8 58 | | | 7 40 | | 1019 | | 1124 | | 1231 | 1 16 | 2 43 | 3 21 | | 4 48 | 5 46 | | | | | 1028 | 1047 |
| 7 | Ilford, for Barking | | | 9 4 | | | 7 48 | | 1025 | | 1130 | | 1237 | 1 22 | 2 49 | 3 27 | | 4 53 | 5 50 | | | | | 1031 | 1054 |
| 9 | Chadwell Heath... | | | 9 10 | | | 7 56 | | 1031 | | | | 1243 | 1 28 | 2 53 | 3 33 | | 4 58 | | | | | | 1038½ | |
| 12 | Romford 1 | | | 9 17 | | | 8 5 | | 1038 | | 1141 | | 1250 | 1 35 | 3 | 3 40 | | 5 6 | | | | | | 10 3 | 1105 |
| 14½ | Harold Wood .. | | | a | | | | | | | | | | | | | | | | | | | | | |
| 17½ | Brentwood ...... | | | 9 30 | | | 8 25 | 9 50 | 1052 | 12 0 | | | 1 3 | 1 52 | 3 15 | 3 52 | | 5 22 | | | | | | 1120 | 1125 |
| 23¾ | Ingatestone ..... | | | | | | 8 40 | 10 1 | | 1213 | | | | 2 5 | | 3 5 | | 5 37 | | | | | | 1134 | |
| 29½ | Chelmsford ..... | | | Stop | | | 8 57 | 1018 | | 1225 | 1238 | Stop | 2 17 | | Stop | | | 5 51 | | | | | | 1150 | |
| 38¾ | Witham Junction 86 | | | | | | 9 22 | 1030 | | | 1255 | | | | | | | | | | | | | 10 8 | |
| 41½ | Kelvedon ...... | | | | | | 9 34 | 1040 | | | 1 4 | | | | | | | 6 5 | | | | | | 1018 | |
| 46¼ | Marks Tey Junc. 86 | 1,2,3 | | | | | 9 46 | | | | 1 16 | | | | | | | 6 19 | | | | | | 1027 | |
| 51¼ | Colchester ...arr | mrn | | | | | 10 4 | 1057 | | | 1 26 | | | | | | | 6 29 | | | | | | 1033 | |
| 52 | Colchester dep | 7 0 | | | | | | | 11 7 | | | 1 30 | | | | | | 5 52 | | | | | | | 1042 |
| 53 | St. Botolph's ... | | | | | | | | 1119 | | | 2 27 | | | | | | 6 17 | | | | | | | |
| 54½ | Hythe ........ | 7 15 | | | | | | | 1123 | | | 2 39 | | | | | | 6 23 | | | | | | | |
| 55½ | Wivenhoe .... | 7 23 | | | | | | | 1131 | | | 3 | | | | | | 6 29 | | | | | | | |
| 61 | Brightlingsea .arr | 7 45 | | | | | | | 1150 | | | 3 10 | | | | | | 6 50 | | | | | | | |
| 57½ | Alresford ...... | Stop | | | | | | | a | | | a | | | | | | a | | | | | | | |
| 59 | Thorington .... | | | | | | | | a | | | 2 54 | | | | | | 6 44 | | | | | | | |
| 60¾ | Bentley Green .. | | | | | | | | 1146 | | | 2 59 | | | | | | 6 49 | | | | | | | |
| 62¾ | Weeley ........ | | | | | | | | 1152 | | | a | | | | | | 6 54 | | | | | | | |
| 64½ | Thorpe ...... | | | | | | | | a | | | a | | | | | | 7 3 | | | | | | | |
| 67 | Kirby Cross.... | | | | | | | | 12 7 | | | a | | | | | | 7 9 | | | | | | | |
| 69½ | Wltn-on-Naze.. | | | | | | | | 1215 | | | 3 20 | | | | | | 7 20 | | | | | | | |
| — | Colchester ...dep | | | | | | | 1012 | 11 0 | | | 1 30 | | | | | | 5 52 5 58 | | | | 1042 | | | 1042 |
| 55½ | Ardleigh ...... | | | | | | | 1026 | | | | a | | | | | | 6 42 | | | | 1030 | | 5 18 | 11 0 |
| 59 | Manningtree... | | | | | | | 1038 | 1117 | | | 1 48 | | | | | | 6 52 6 15 | | | | | | 5 23 | 11 0 |
| — | Manningtree d | | | | 9 10 | 1125 | | | | | | 1 55 | | | | | | 6 26 | | | | | | 5 35 | |
| 60½ | Mistley ...... | | | | 9 15 | 1130 | | | | | | a | | | | | | 6 31 | | | | 1130 | | 5 40 | |
| 62 | Bradfield .... | | | | a | a | | | | | | a | | | | | | a | | | | | | a | |
| 67¾ | Wrabness .... | | | | a | a | | | | | | a | | | | | | a | | | | | | a | |
| 69½ | Dovercourt... | | | | 9 57 | 1157 | | | | | | 2 27 | | | | | | 6 57 | | | | 1135 | | 6 7 | 1135 |
| 69¾ | Harwich ...arr | 1,2,3 | | | 10 0 | 12 0 | | | | | | 2 30 | | | | | | 7 0 | | | | 1140 | | 6 11 | 1140 |
| 62½ | Bentley Junction | mrn | | | | 1050 | | | | | | 1 56 | | | | | | 6 1 | | | | 1032 | | 5 38 | |
| — | Bentley ☞ dp | | | | 9 0 | 1055 | | | | | | 2 0 | | | | | | 6 5 | | | | | | | |
| 69½ | Hadleigh ...arr | | | | 9 25 | 1120 | 1,2,3 | | | | | 2 25 | | | | | | 6 42 | | | | | | | |
| 68 | Ipswich ......arr | Stop | | | mrn | 1110 | 1137 | | | | | 2 13 | | | | | | 6 18 6 35 | | | | 1125 | | | 1125 |
| — | Ipswich ......dep | Stop | | | 7 10 | | 1150 | | | | | 2 23 | | | | | | 6 45 | | | | | | | |
| 71½ | Westerfield ... | | | | 7 20 | | 12 0 | | | | | a | | | | | | 6 55 | | | | | | | |
| 75½ | Bealings ...... | | | | 7 29 | | 12 12 | | | | | a | | | | | | 7 4 | | | | | | | |
| 78½ | Woodbridge ... | | | | 7 38 | | 1218 | | | | | 2 39 | | | | | | 7 12 | | | | | | | |
| 79¾ | Melton ...... | | | | 7 43 | | 1223 | | | | 1,2,3 | a | | | | | | 7 16 | | | | | | | |
| 83½ | Wickham Mkt.J | | | | 7 54 | | 1233 | | | | aft | 3 1 | | | | | | 7 26 | | | | | | | |
| 85½ | Wickhm Mkt. J | | | 8 0 | | 1240 | | | | | | 5 20 | | | | | | 7 58 | | | | | | | |
| 88 | Marlesford .. | | | 8 8 | | 1247 | | Thurs. only. | | | { | 3 12 | | | | | | 5 28 | | | 8 3 | | | | |
| 88 | Parham ...... | | | 8 16 | | 1257 | | | | | { | 2 37 | | | | | | 5 37 | | | 8 7 | | | | |
| 90½ | Framlinghm | | | 8 25 | | 1 5 | | | | | | 2 30 | | | | | | 5 45 | | | 8 23 | | | | |
| | | 1 | 2 | 3 | 4 | 5 | 6 | 7 | 8 | 9 | 10 | 11 | 12 | 13 | 14 | 15 | 16 | 17 | 18 | 19 | 20 | 21 | 22 |

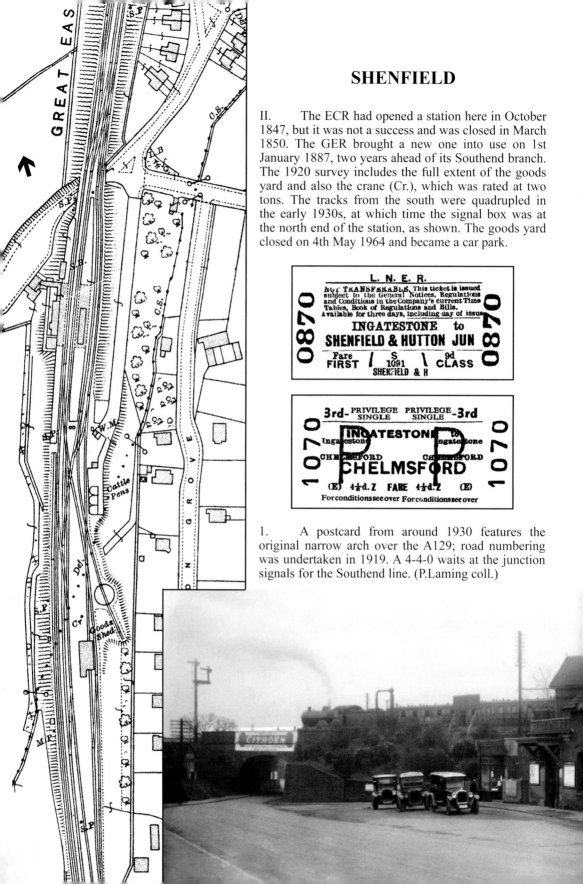

# SHENFIELD

II.      The ECR had opened a station here in October 1847, but it was not a success and was closed in March 1850. The GER brought a new one into use on 1st January 1887, two years ahead of its Southend branch. The 1920 survey includes the full extent of the goods yard and also the crane (Cr.), which was rated at two tons. The tracks from the south were quadrupled in the early 1930s, at which time the signal box was at the north end of the station, as shown. The goods yard closed on 4th May 1964 and became a car park.

1.      A postcard from around 1930 features the original narrow arch over the A129; road numbering was undertaken in 1919. A 4-4-0 waits at the junction signals for the Southend line. (P.Laming coll.)

2.      Three platforms sufficed until 1934, when an additional island platform was added on the extreme right. Class F6 2-4-2T no. 7230 is about to start its journey to Liverpool Street, sometime in September 1949. (R.F.Roberts/SLS coll.)

3.      Waiting to leave for Liverpool Street on the same occasion is class J15 0-6-0 no. 5464. This was the limit of electric services from London at that time. The train is the 4.11pm Saturdays-only from Maldon. (R.F.Roberts/SLS coll.)

4. The term "& Hutton" was applied from 1887 until 1969. Class B17 4-6-0 no. 61672 *West Ham United* is speeding through on 23rd July 1955 with the 2.50pm Clacton to Liverpool Street express. (H.Ballantyne)

➜ 5. Standing at platform No. 5 sometime in 1956 are two new four-coach sets of class 306 on test. 06 was the unit number and the small S that follows the number indicated that Southend was its route. (BR/D.Brennand coll.)

➜ 6. The west facade is seen in August 1961. It had been completed in 1934 at the time of the provision of steel spans for the bridges over the road. (BR/D.Brennand coll.)

7.     This view towards London includes four of the five platforms, part of a bridge span, the signal box and the upper parts of the three lift shafts. The box was in use from December 1933 until May 1981. (R.F.Roberts/SLS coll.)

8.     The panel came into use in 1981 and has the quadruple track from London on the left. Lower right is the up line from Southend and less clear is the down one. The Southend flyunder line crosses the diagram. The panel was in use until 30th August 1993, when Liverpool Street took over the area. (D.Pollock)

9.　　A class 321 stands at platform No. 3 on 14th March 1997. These EMUs were built at York in 1988-90 and were used on long distance services. All five platforms will take 12 coaches. (F.Hornby)

10.　　Seen on the same day is the new entrance building from the 1970s. The bridge (left) and the platform structures remained unchanged. The name "Great Eastern" once again adorns the frontage. (F.Hornby)

11.     A stopping service to Liverpool Street was photographed at platform No. 4 on 25th April 2004. No. 315818 was one of a large class also built at York in 1979-80 for suburban work on this route. (B.I.Nathan)

12.     No. 90007 is propelling a train to Norwich on 18th June 2005 and is accelerating it from platform No. 3. The four tracks from London become two for Chelmsford and two for Southend Victoria. (B.I.Nathan)

13.     The Southend flyunder was provided in 1934 and it allowed down trains to pass under the main line. Class B12/3 4-6-0 no. 61546 hauls a Liverpool Street to Southend-on-Sea train and is approaching Mountnessing Junction on 10th May 1952. (B.Morrison)

**Other views of this station can be found in**
*Branch Lines to Southend and Southminster* **and** *Ilford to Shenfield.*

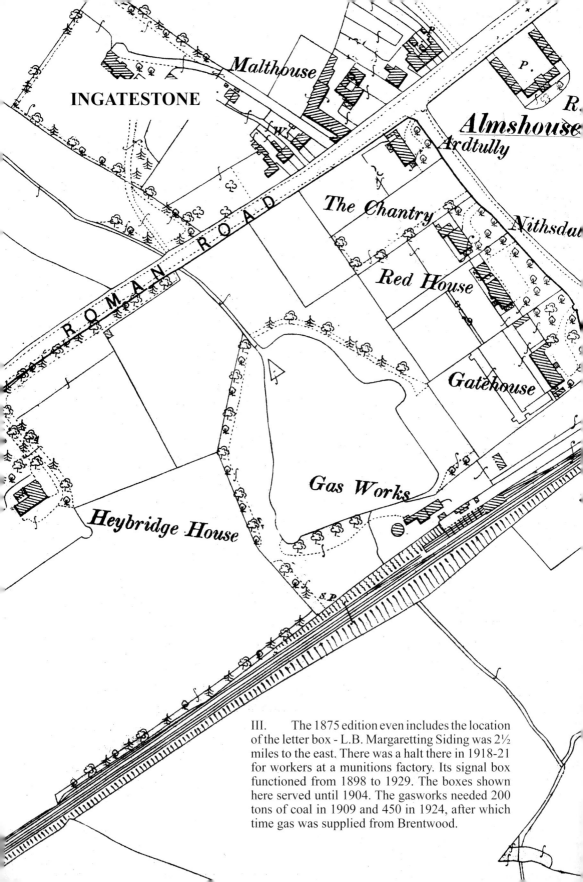

**INGATESTONE**

Malthouse

Almshouse

Ardtully

ROMAN ROAD

The Chantry

Nithsda

Red House

Gatehouse

Gas Works

Heybridge House

III.     The 1875 edition even includes the location of the letter box - L.B. Margaretting Siding was 2½ miles to the east. There was a halt there in 1918-21 for workers at a munitions factory. Its signal box functioned from 1898 to 1929. The boxes shown here served until 1904. The gasworks needed 200 tons of coal in 1909 and 450 in 1924, after which time gas was supplied from Brentwood.

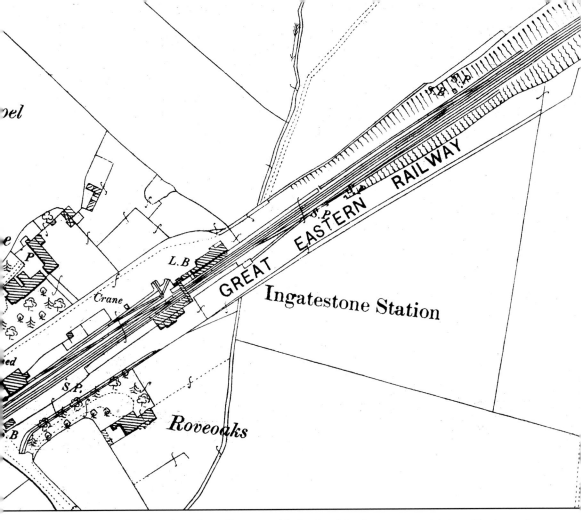

14.　　Prolonged and acrimonious disputes with the local landowner meant intermittent opening of two platforms in Stock Lane and tickets being issued at the Almshouse. The present site came into use sometime in 1846 and the sidings followed. This view is right from the join of the pages. (P.Laming coll.)

15.    We move closer to the down side building, the up one being seen beyond the 30cwt crane. The gate posts on the left are at the entrance to the main part of the goods yard. The Tudor styling was demanded by the landowner. (P.Laming coll.)

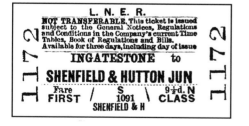

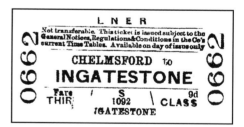

16.    We now move to the right, some years later, and examine the 1885 up side building and the rear of a down train. The population was 1748 in 1901 and 3549 in 1961. Thoby signal box was west of the station from 1898 until 1937. (Lens of Sutton coll.)

17.    The footbridge lost its roof before electrification and gained safety barriers thereafter. This view towards London shows the siding to the goods shed. Freight traffic ceased here on 4th October 1965. (Lens of Sutton coll.)

→18.  A view towards Chelmsford includes the signal box, which was still in place on 11th April 2011, together with a down loop. It was electrified and its eastern points were to the left of the camera. (D.Pollock)

→19.  The loop is lower right on the diagram; both main lines are signalled for reversible running. Despite the many levers, all signals are colour light. The frame closed on 20th October 1996 and was replaced by a switch panel for the crossing. (D.Pollock)

20.	A view from the signal box features two class 86 electric locomotives, with an empty container wagon behind. The train is running from Felixstowe to Stratford and then on to Coatbridge, in Scotland on 8th May 2001. (D.Pollock)

21.	Seen from the level crossing on the same day is no. 315812, which is bound for Liverpool Street forming the 07.52 from Chelmsford. It is substituting for a class 321 unit. Colour light signalling was installed as far as Chelmsford as early as 1937. (D.Pollock)

# WEST OF CHELMSFORD

22.    A Norwich to Liverpool Street train is hauled over the River Can by a class 47 diesel on 13th October 1977. Cromptons Siding was to the west and it had a signal box from 1897 to 1937. (T.Heavyside)

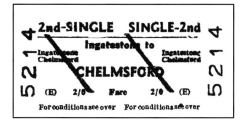

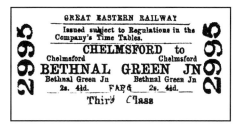

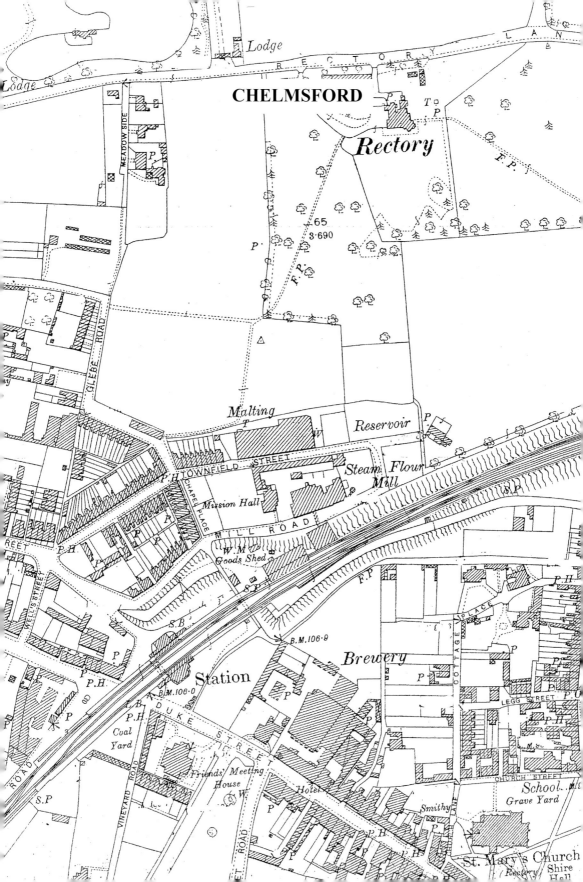

# CHELMSFORD

*Rectory*

*Lodge*

*Lodge*

RECTORY LANE

F.P.

65
3·690

P.

P.

F.P.

MEADOW SIDE

GLEBE ROAD

*Malting*

*Reservoir*

*Steam Flour Mill*

P.H TOWNFIELD STREET

CHAPEL PLACE

*Mission Hall*

MILL ROAD

W.M Goods Shed

S.B.

B.M.106·9

F.P.

WELL'S STREET

P.H.

S.B.

*Brewery*

COTTAGE PLACE

LEGG STREET

P.H.

P.U

*Station*

B.M.106·0

DUKE STREET

VINEYARD ROAD

Coal Yard

*Friends' Meeting House*

*Hotel*

*Smithy*

CHURCH STREET

*School*

*Grave Yard*

S.P.

ROAD

S.P.

*St. Mary's Church*
*Rectory*
*Shire Hall*

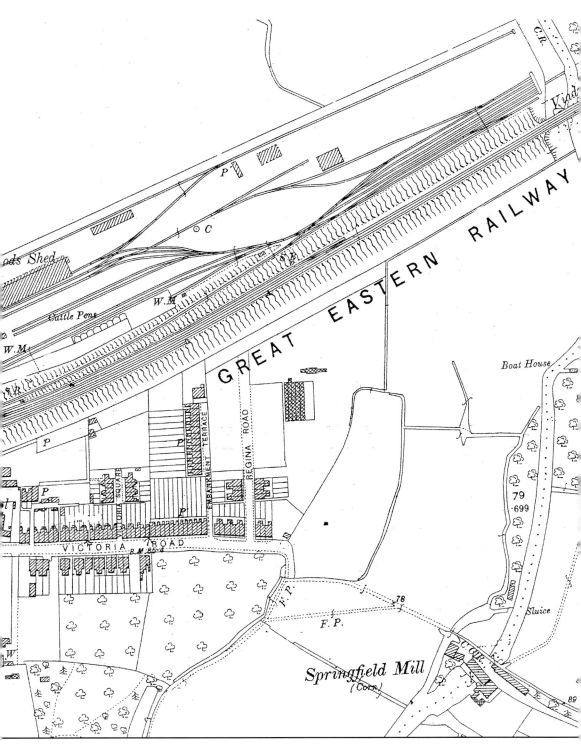

IV.     The 1897 edition at 20ins to 1 mile has the River Chelmer on the right and much of the main line on an embankment in order to cross the valley. The part on the left is on a viaduct, almost 300yds in length. The goods yard (right page) was laid out in the late 1870s, with a steep incline down from the main line. Its box is above the school.

23.     The main building was completed on the up side of the line in 1856 and is seen in about 1912. Slip coaches from down trains had been introduced in 1872. The bus is GER property. (P.Laming coll.)

24.     This westward panorama has the signal box above the down platform canopy. The first station had been near the centre of the map and it had an island platform. (P.Laming coll.)

25.     A locomotive depot was established in 1883, close to the viaduct. All that was provided was a pit (left), a messroom (right) and a water tank. One or two engines were based here, with three crews and a night cleaner. Class N7 0-6-2Ts are resting on 12th July 1958. The depot faded away with dieselisation in about 1960 and the last steam working was in September 1962. (K.Fairey/Colour-Rail.com)

26.     The centre road was useful for terminating trains to layover or, as in this case, an Ipswich bound parcels train to be set aside. (Lens of Sutton coll.)

27.     Moving to the east end of the up platform in the early 1960s, we see the commencement of the long berthing siding, which was also electrified in 1956. (Lens of Sutton coll.)

28.      The connecting spur to Lower Yard is on the right in this eastward view from 4th October 1981. There had earlier been an 8-ton crane and there was a total of seven private sidings in the area. (G.Fitch)

29.      The 1856 building on the up side remained well conserved to be photographed on 24th June 1984. Little had changed 25 years later. The population rose from 12,580 in 1901 to 52,230 in 1961 and by 1986 there were around 16,000 passengers on each work day. (B.W.L.Brooksbank)

30.     A GPO terminal was established in Lower Yard on 19th January 1987 and fork lift trucks were used to load the mailbags through the wide train doorways, which had roller shutters. No. 302991 is leaving the only electrified siding on 12th December 1990, destined for Liverpool Street. No. 47615 forms the 16.05 Postmail to Norwich. Rowntree's had a massive shed nearby to facilitate the loading of VDA vans. Lafarge opened a stone terminal here in May 1989, the siding being electrified in its initial years. Only this one was in use in 2011. (Dr. I C.Scotchman)

31.     The signal box was photographed internally and externally on 16th October 1996. The white levers are those out of use. The box had opened in 1899 and can also be seen in picture 32. (D.Pollock)

32.    This is our only view of some of the arches which make up Chelmsford Viaduct. The box closed on 20th October 1996, but was still in place in 2011. (D.Pollock)

33.    No. 86234 *Suffolk - Relax, Refresh, Return* pushes the 12.30 Liverpool Street to Norwich out of the down platform on 28th March 2005. The name "Anglia" was obsolete by that time. (D.Pollock)

# HATFIELD PEVEREL

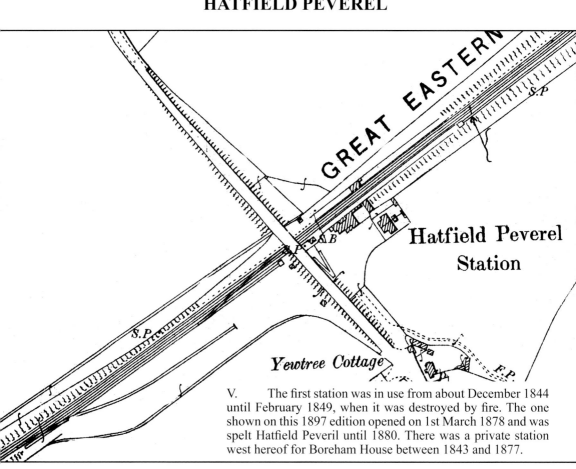

V.     The first station was in use from about December 1844 until February 1849, when it was destroyed by fire. The one shown on this 1897 edition opened on 1st March 1878 and was spelt Hatfield Peveril until 1880. There was a private station west hereof for Boreham House between 1843 and 1877.

34.     The footbridge arrived in the Edwardian era and is seen from the south on a postcard from that period. To the west, there had been signal boxes at Chantry and New Hall until September 1961. (P.Laming coll.)

35.     The road had been diverted slightly, its original alignment being on that of the footbridge. This eastward view has one of the two goods sidings on the right and the down refuge siding on the left. (P.Laming coll.)

36.     Glimpsed in the previous photograph, the signal box had been positioned to allow the signalman to supervise passengers using the foot crossing, prior to the provision of a footbridge. The box was in use from 1913 until 17th September 1961. (P.Laming coll.)

37.    A view in the other direction reveals unusual spacing for the uninsulated telephone wires and a rather frost prone water tank on the facilities for gentlemen. (SLS coll.)

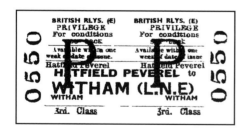

38.     The gents had gone from the down platform by the 1960s, but electric lighting had arrived. The platforms were soon to be raised and lengthened to take 12 cars. (Lens of Sutton coll.)

39.     Barrows confirm that parcels were still conveyed in that era, but general goods traffic ceased on 27th June 1960. The population rose from 1208 in 1901 to 2850 in 1961. (Lens of Sutton coll.)

40. The eastward panorama in October 1994 includes tasteful new lighting and the latest information screens. In the distance had been Blunts Hall signal box until 17th September 1961. (B.W.L.Brooksbank)

41. The southeast elevation was recorded on the same day and the high standard of restoration must be admired; even the chimney pots had been retained or replaced.
(B.W.L.Brooksbank)

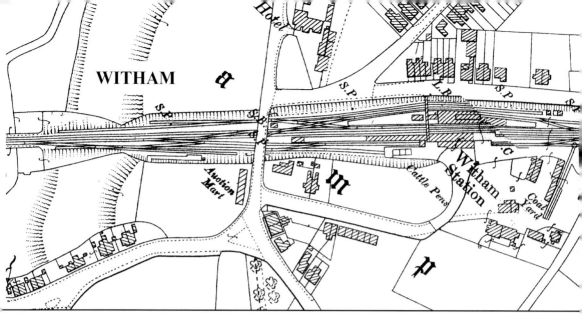

WITHAM

Auction
Mart

Witham
Station

Cattle Pens

Coal
Yard

VI.　　The 1897 survey has the Braintree branch at the top and the Maldon one at the bottom. The right part of the triangle was out of use by that time and is disconnected at its north end, which was termed Witham East.

42.　　This is the south elevation of the building shown on the map. The roof of the footbridge can be seen on the left. There was only one up platform and when it became an island platform, the building was destroyed. (P.Laming coll.)

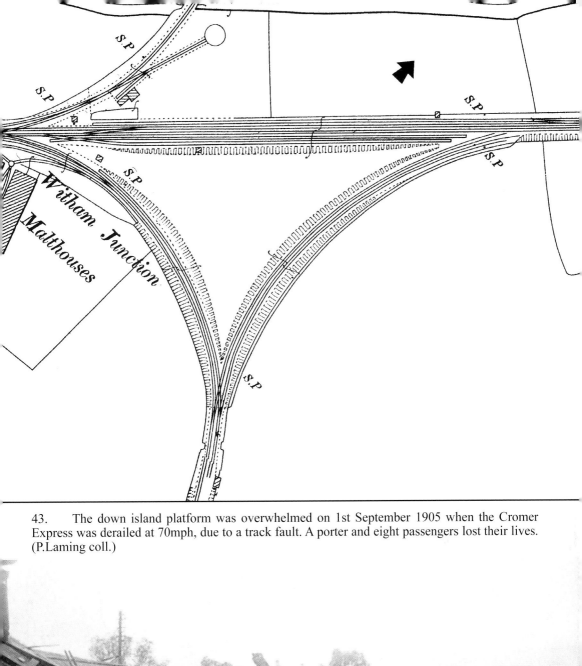

S.P.

S.P.

S.P.

S.P.

S.P.

S.P.

S.P.

*Witham Junction*

*Malthouses*

43.    The down island platform was overwhelmed on 1st September 1905 when the Cromer Express was derailed at 70mph, due to a track fault. A porter and eight passengers lost their lives. (P.Laming coll.)

44.     An unusual Christmas card was produced by an enterprising printer in the early 20th century. Junction Box can be found on the map at the join of the pages. It was in use from 1909 until 8th May 1960. The other box was simply "Witham" and is on the left page, above the Auction Mart. Witham East Box is not shown; its dates were about 1891-1926. (P.Laming coll.)

45.     An eastward panorama from the same period shows the new entrance and booking office on the north side of the station. It was built above the loop used mainly by the Braintree branch trains. (P.Laming coll.)

46.     Running between the malthouses and the signal box is an up express on 16th February 1952. It is hauled by no. 70000 *Britannia*, a 4-6-2 of a type introduced to the route by BR in 1951. The final two shunting horses here retired in April 1954. (A.J.Pike/F.Hornby coll.)

47.     A view towards London on 26th May 1956 includes a Maldon branch train standing at the 1907 platform. Halfway to Kelvedon, there was an intermediate signal box called Rivenhall. (H.C.Casserley)

48.	Looking in the other direction on the same day, we find a freight train recessed in the Braintree loop. The goods yard is on the right and this closed on 7th December 1981. (R.M.Casserley)

49.	The Braintree service was operated by class F6 2-4-2T no. 67228 on 25th August 1956. The two small cylinders form the Westinghouse pump for the air brakes. (B.Pask)

50.　　Both branch services were provided mainly by diesel railbuses from July 1958. This example waits to leave for Maldon in August 1964. Each car seated 56 and had only two axles. (B.Pask)

51. No. 312789 was working a Clacton to Liverpool Street service on 30th August 1982, while a Braintree train waits on the left. The latter branch had been electrified on 3rd October 1977. (T.Heavyside)

52. Waiting under the booking office on the same day is no. 312795; it is bound for Braintree. The Maldon branch had lost its passenger service on 7th September 1964 and public freight traffic ceased on 18th April 1966. (T.Heavyside)

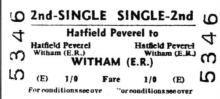

53. No. 86227 speeds through on 22nd March 2003, pushing a Liverpool Street to Norwich service. The photographer allows us to enjoy the intricate valence and the art form of the stanchion brackets. (T.Heavyside)

→ 54. A footbridge extension southwards to the car park was authorised in 2011. We look west as no. 170207 waits to depart. These DMUs were introduced in 1998 and were used on a service between here and Basingstoke until 2002. They also ran from Peterborough, plus the East Suffolk line, to London. This is the 11.00 Lowestoft to Liverpool Street on 25th May 2005; the Peterborough via Ely service continued until December 2010. (D.Pollock)

→ 55. Our final view of this interesting station is from the same day and includes the junction signals for the down loop, plus the modernised maltings. The former are controlled from Liverpool Street. No. 66705 *Nene Valley* is roaring in that direction, but will turn off at Stratford and run to Hams Hall, Birmingham. On the right is the panel box, which was in use until 25th May 1997. After the Ipswich Tunnel Blockade (see caption 118) in Summer 2004, such trains could run from Felixstowe to the West Coast Main Line via Stratford and the North London Line with 'High Cube' containers (9ft 6ins) on standard height wagons. Prior to this, Low Floor or Pocket wagons could be used either via London or cross country to carry 'High Cube' containers, the problem being that these wagons had a lower payload and cost more to rent. Compare the leading container with the one behind to see the difference in height. (D.Pollock)

> **Other pictures of the locations can be seen in**
> *Branch Lines around Witham and Kelvedon.*

# KELVEDON

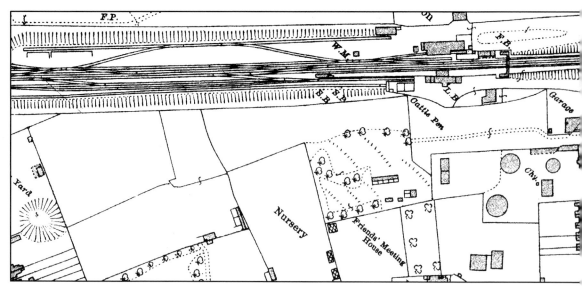

VII.    The 1923 extract is just north of the town centre and has the main line station on the left page and the branch one on the right. Near the page boundary is Station Road and the River Blackwater, which runs roughly parallel to the main line from Witham.

56.    Passengers arriving on foot would walk up the hill beside the house, from Station Road. To the left of the dwelling (which was for the station master) is the footbridge to the down platform and beyond it is the footway to the Low Level station, for trains to Tollesbury. (P.Laming coll.)

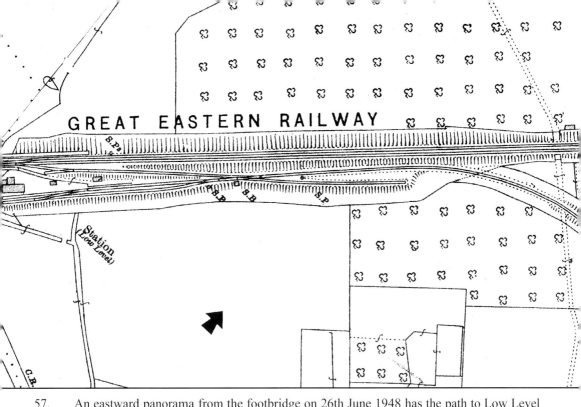

GREAT EASTERN RAILWAY

Station
(Low Level)

57.    An eastward panorama from the footbridge on 26th June 1948 has the path to Low Level starting at the end of the up platform. It passes over Station Road and also the river before descending to the branch platform. The connecting line drops at 1 in 50. (H.C.Casserley)

58.     This view towards London from about 1958 includes the inclined approach roads to both platforms. The goods yard is in the distance, together with its spacious shed, in part. The signal box can also be glimpsed, below the up side canopy. It closed on 3rd December 1961. The warehouse was that of Kings Seeds for many years. (D.Thompson/D.Brennand coll.)

59.     Service for passengers on the branch was withdrawn on 7th May 1951, but freight continued to Tiptree until 1st October 1962, mainly for jam. (D.Trevor Rowe)

60.     The still busy goods yard was recorded not long before its closure on 7th December 1964. Its unusual crane was rated at 30cwt. Rivenhall signal box had been in the distance between about 1899 and 1961. (Lens of Sutton coll.)

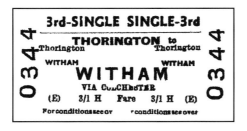

61.     Nos 312788 and 312796 are bound for ➜     62.   Seen on the same day is no. 309602
Liverpool Street on 12th August 1986. Many   working an up train under the footbridge, which
such low canopies suffered from air turbulence   was erected just prior to electrification. An increased
as passing train speeds increased. (A.Ingram)   clearance for the wires was required. (A.Ingram)

➜    63. No. 86227 *Golden Jubilee* rushes through on 22nd March and passes the new building
on its way from Norwich to London. These Bo-Bo locomotives were built in 1965-66 by BR and
English Electric. The new building was completed in 1990. (T.Heavyside)

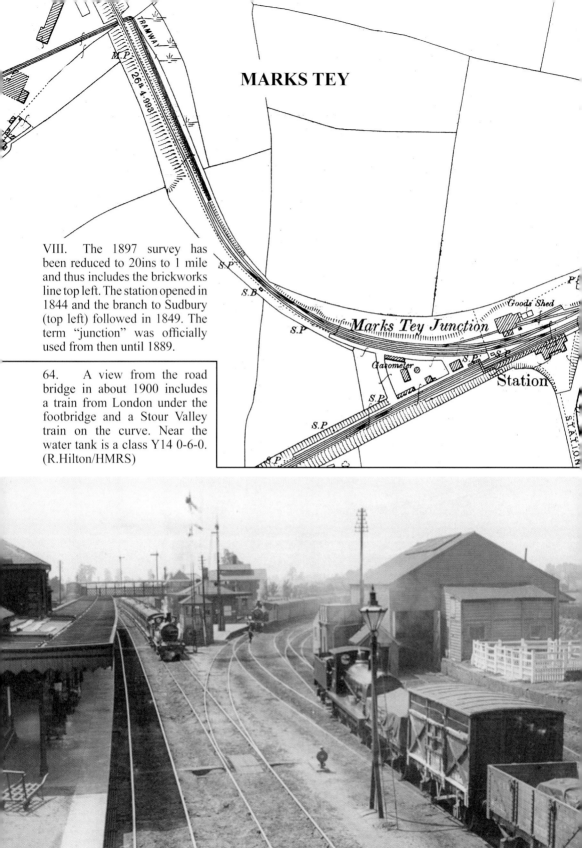

# MARKS TEY

VIII. The 1897 survey has been reduced to 20ins to 1 mile and thus includes the brickworks line top left. The station opened in 1844 and the branch to Sudbury (top left) followed in 1849. The term "junction" was officially used from then until 1889.

64. A view from the road bridge in about 1900 includes a train from London under the footbridge and a Stour Valley train on the curve. Near the water tank is a class Y14 0-6-0. (R.Hilton/HMRS)

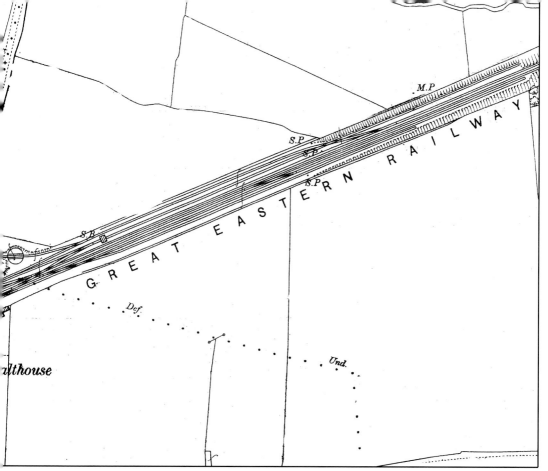

65.     The road bridge is just beyond the right border of this postcard view from around 1910. There were regular slip coaches from down trains until July 1939, the last on the route being from the 4.57pm from Liverpool Street. (P.Laming coll.)

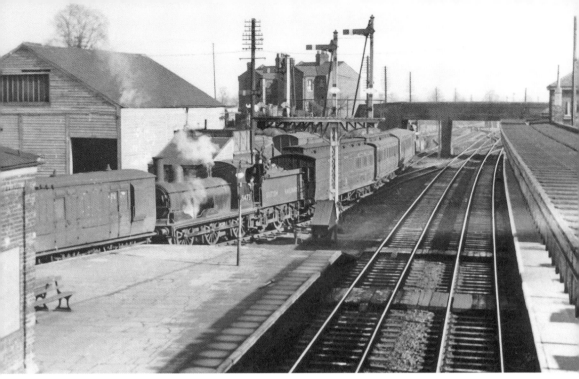

66.    Staff dwellings are in the background in this record of a Colne Valley train being shunted on 19th February 1949 by class J15 0-6-0 no. 65473. The size of the goods shed is impressive from this angle. (J.H.Meredith)

67.    We are on the up platform on 26th May 1956 and the LNER style electric lighting is evident. It is curious that a canopy was not provided on the down side. The down train is headed by class B1 no. 61227, a 4-6-0 type introduced in 1942. (H.C.Casserley)

68.    Class E4 2-4-0 no. 62789 has three coaches in tow on 20th March 1957, as it works from Colchester to Cambridge, with a good head of steam. (B.Jennings)

69.    The 2.01pm Colchester to Cambridge was hauled by class B17/4 4-6-0 no. 61651 on 23rd August 1958. The goods yard seems empty, but it did not close until November 1963. (K.Fairey/Colour-Rail.com)

70.     A sense of anticipation was recorded on the Sudbury platform on 30th June 1979, by which time the goods yard was being adapted as a car park. (R.F.Roberts/SLS coll.)

71.     No. E0593 is working the 13.57 Sudbury to Colchester on the same day. Trains ceased to run north of Sudbury in 1967 and the Colne Valley Line closed in 1965. Most Sudbury trains have terminated here. (R.F.Roberts/SLS coll.)

72.     The signal box is in the distance and the down loop was near to it. No. 90149 heads a Freightliner from Felixstowe to Crewe on 16th April 1992. It will run via the North London Line. (M.Turvey)

73.     No. 86230 *The Duke of Wellington* is hauling the 17.18 Ipswich to Liverpool Street on 17th August 1993, while stock is berthed on the right. The signal box closed on 18th October 1997. The two boxes on the map lasted until 1926. (M.Turvey)

← 74. The up sidings were altered to form a loop with two parallel sidings for the Tarmac Sand Terminal. No. 60006 *Scunthorpe Ironmaster* is ready with a loaded train. The traffic began on 19th November 1969, the sand being brought two miles by road and then taken to Mile End. This train is destined for Hayes & Harlington Tarmac Siding on 24th March 1999. (D.Pollock)

# WEST OF COLCHESTER

75. We look towards the station from a signal post in January 1960 and see the marshalling yard on the left. The route was soon to be straightened to allow speeds to be increased from 40 to 90mph. Work on the scheme had started before World War II, with some of the sidings on the right being taken out of use. Behind us had been Lexden signal box until 1927 and Stanway until 1961. (HMRS)

# COLCHESTER

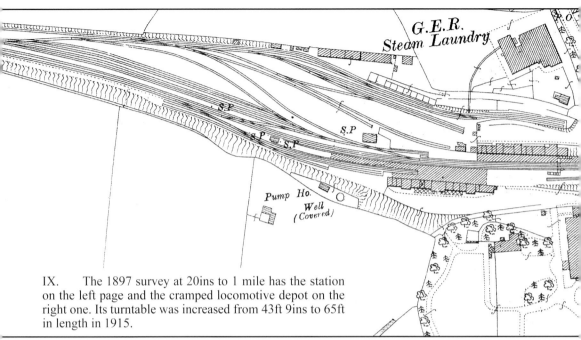

IX.    The 1897 survey at 20ins to 1 mile has the station on the left page and the cramped locomotive depot on the right one. Its turntable was increased from 43ft 9ins to 65ft in length in 1915.

76.    This westward panorama from the signal box has the asylum on the left and the up side building in line with the telegraph poles. The latter structure was erected in 1865 and much of it survives today. The 18 private sidings of 1929 were reduced to 11 by 1956. All have long gone. (P.Laming coll.)

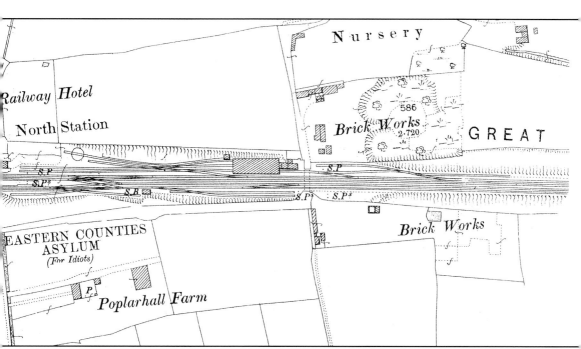

Railway Hotel

North Station

EASTERN COUNTIES
ASYLUM
*(For Idiots)*

Poplarhall Farm

N u r s e r y

Brick Works
586
2·720

G R E A T

Brick Works

77.    On the right is the goods shed, which postdates the map. Arriving from Marks Tey and rounding the curve is class E4 2-4-0T no. 62789, sometime in the 1950s. The goods yard closed on 18th April 1966. The signal box functioned from 1888 until 18th September 1960 and a successor to this and Junction Box was in use until 4th December 1983. (R.F.Roberts/SLS coll.)

78.     The first engine shed was replaced in 1891 by the one shown on the map, which had three roads. The new shed, seen in July 1956, was built by the LNER in 1930-31, but it was inadequate for the 61 locomotives then allocated. Official closure of the dilapidated premises was 2nd November 1959. (H.C.Casserley)

79.     We are looking towards Ipswich from the end of the up platform in the late 1950s, with the outline of the engine shed in the distance. Engines often queued for repair, this frequently having to be undertaken in the open at this congested location. (Lens of Sutton coll.)

80.    We move to the London end of the up platform and gasp at the curvature, which was operationally very inconvenient. The water tank received its supply from the local water company, not from the nearest river, which was often the case elsewhere. Trains running via Sudbury usually terminated in the bay on the right, although some continued to St. Botolphs.
(R.F.Roberts/SLS coll.)

81. The yard outside the engine shed was always busy, as witnessed on 10th July 1955 with class N7 0-6-2T no. 69700 and class B12 4-6-0 no. 61561 facing us. A class J19 is in the middle. (D.Brennand coll.)

↓ 82. Obscuring the locomotive depot on 24th May 1958 is 4-6-0 class B17/6 no. 61648 *Arsenal*. On the right is Junction Box, which was in use from 1921 until 4th February 1962. The last coach is near the last span. The population increased from 38,373 in 1901 to 67,430 in 1961. (F.Hornby)

↑ 83. The 1959-62 rebuilding resulted in the unusual facility of an inset platform (No. 4) recessed into the up main (No. 3). This arrangement allows a slow train or a Clacton service to be overtaken by a London train and connections provided. The bay platform was the only one to have a wire during the 25kV trials in around 1960. (Lens of Sutton coll.)

X.     The flyunder for the down Clacton route was completed in 1962 and this line was the only one on this diagram not to have bidirectional running east of the platforms, thereafter.

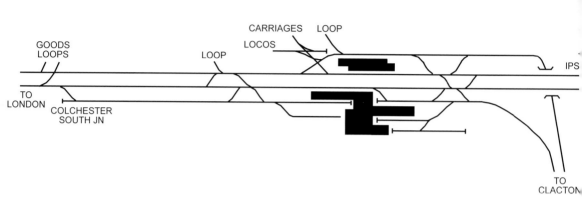

84.     No. 309627 is at No. 3 in June 1969 and is working a Clacton to London service. These units were much admired, but the curved front windows presented problems and were replaced with flat ones. This class was introduced in 1961 as two-car sets for that route. Most were reformed as four-car units and were a great success. (Colour-Rail.com)

85.     The 11.30 Liverpool Street to Norwich was headed by no. 47009 on 13th October 1977. Seen from platform 4, the locomotive is on the bridge over the road, as are platforms 4 and 5. (T.Heavyside)

86.     A diesel depot was built west of the station in 1959 and it is seen in October 1987, from the east. North of it, a compound was created for overhead line equipment and also five carriage sidings, with a washing plant, plus the 1983 panel box. Included are nos 47341 and 03059. (D.C.Pearce)

87.    The multitude of sidings include several for the permanent way engineers and this short one near the diesel depot for improvised snow ploughs. They were quite often used on the Clacton branch with two class 37 diesels. The photograph is from 11th May 1989, as is the next one. (A.C.Mott)

88.    During the rebuilding around 1960, an extra entrance was provided, adjacent to a new car park on the north side. The down platform became an island and was given all new buildings. The curve soon divides to join the up and down goods loops, the latter connecting with two reception roads. (A.C.Mott)

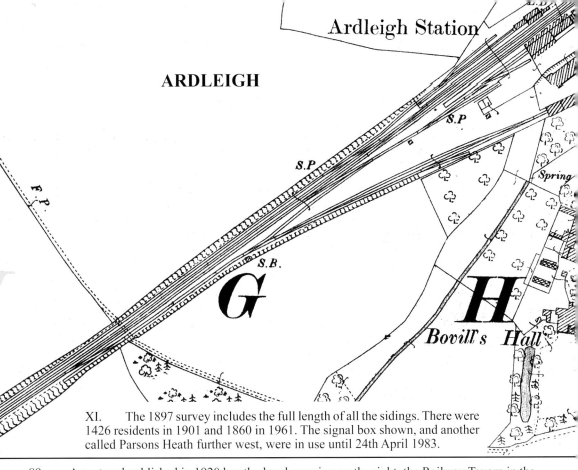

# ARDLEIGH

Ardleigh Station

*S.P.*

*Spring*

*S.P.*

*S.P.*

*F.P.*

*S.B.*

*G*

*H*

*Bovill's Hall*

XI. The 1897 survey includes the full length of all the sidings. There were 1426 residents in 1901 and 1860 in 1961. The signal box shown, and another called Parsons Heath further west, were in use until 24th April 1983.

89. A postcard published in 1920 has the level crossing on the right, the Railway Tavern in the background and the house for the station master on the left. (P.Laming coll.)

90.     A typical GER train arrives at the down platform before it was raised. The approach path is unusually well protected by the building on the right and the sign on it states PASSENGERS ARE CAUTIONED NOT TO CROSS THE LINE. (P.Laming coll.)

91.     A panorama from the level crossing shows improved ballasting and the foot crossing not to be used. A one-ton crane was recorded here in 1938, it being in the goods shed. (Dr. J.Westhall/A.Vaughan coll.)

92.    A view towards Ipswich includes the stylish goods shed in which much horticultural and seed traffic was handled. The goods service was withdrawn on 7th December 1964. (P.Laming coll.)

93.    Judging by the weeds and lack of fencing, this photograph was probably taken about the time of closure to passengers, which was 6th November 1967. However, two signs are still to be seen. (C.Nash coll.)

# MANNINGTREE

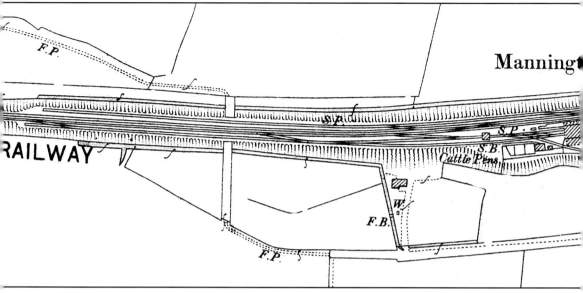

XII.     The 1897 survey has the 1854 Harwich branch on the right; the eastern part of the triangular junction did not open until 29th August 1882. It is known by railway staff as North Curve. Three signal boxes are shown; there were two more at the other apexes of the triangle. The gasworks was using 200 tons of coal in 1901, 2000 in 1938 and 3000 in 1945. It was in use in 1860 until 1950.

94.     We look from the road which is lower right on the map and find Station Hotel in the centre and the station itself in the distance. The houses postdate the map. The local population was 872 in 1901 and 524 in 1961. (P.Laming coll.)

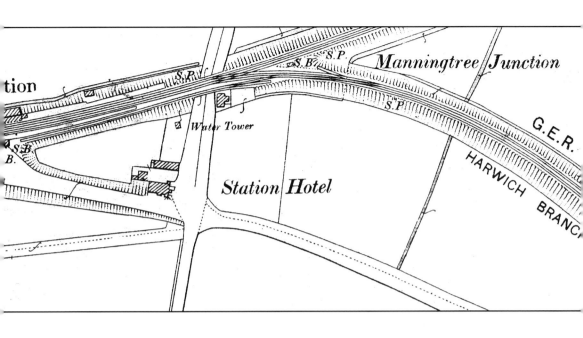

95.　　Approaching from Ipswich is "Britannia" class 4-6-0 no. 70012 *John of Gaunt*. This locomotive often ran more than 10,000 miles per month. There was an underpass parallel to the level crossing, but it has limited headroom. Its walls are in the right foreground. Prior to World War II, sidings were listed for Brantham (a village two miles northwards) and for British Xylonite and Keeble, who had private ones. (Dr J.Westhall/A.Vaughan coll.)

96.     South Junction Box is seen from the east end of the up platform. It closed on 27th September 1984. The map shows the box to have been on the other side of the main line in the 19th century. North Junction box lasted until 1925, the connection having been controlled remotely ever since. The photograph is from 7th January 1980. (D.C.Pearce)

97.     All the down starting signals are evident as a class 40 1Co-Co1 diesel accelerates east. This type was introduced in 1958. (Dr. J.Westhall/A.Vaughan coll.)

98.     The down side was well protected at this often draughty location, although the subway entrances are remote from the canopies. The dormer window adds charm. Sadly, the canopy was later lost. (Lens of Sutton coll.)

99.     An InterCity service to London makes connection with a DMU from Harwich on 8th October 1977, when the car park in the station approach had limited use and the trains included a buffet. From 1986, many branch trains terminated here, the others running to Colchester. (R.F.Roberts/SLS coll.)

➜     100.    The up siding serving the former goods yard is on the left. Freight traffic ceased in July 1966. No. 47006 approaches with the 11.30 Liverpool Street to Norwich on 19th May 1977. "Brighton Belle" no. 3054 awaits an uncertain future; 35 years later a unit was being reassembled in original formation. (B.Morrison)

➜     101. No. 37049 is signalled for Ipswich on 7th January 1980, as three new signals await commissioning. New platform lighting is also evident. The train will soon pass the site of Brantham siding, which had a signal box until 15th February 1930. (D.C.Pearce)

102.    It is 4th December 2001 and Anglia Railways Driving Brake Standard Open coach no. 9704 leads a down London Liverpool Street - Norwich service. It has always been operational policy since the introduction of push-pull working on the main line to place the locomotive at the London end. In the background is fellow class 86 no. 86252 *Sheppard 100* which was dumped here in the down siding after suffering fire damage at Ardleigh. (D.Pollock)

# EAST OF MANNINGTREE

103.    Ex-Southern Railway class S15 no. 841 together with diesel no. 31125 head a special train across the first of two viaducts on 15th October 1977. The county boundary is near its centre. This is the River Stour Viaduct and the other is called Cattawade Viaduct. (T.Heavyside)

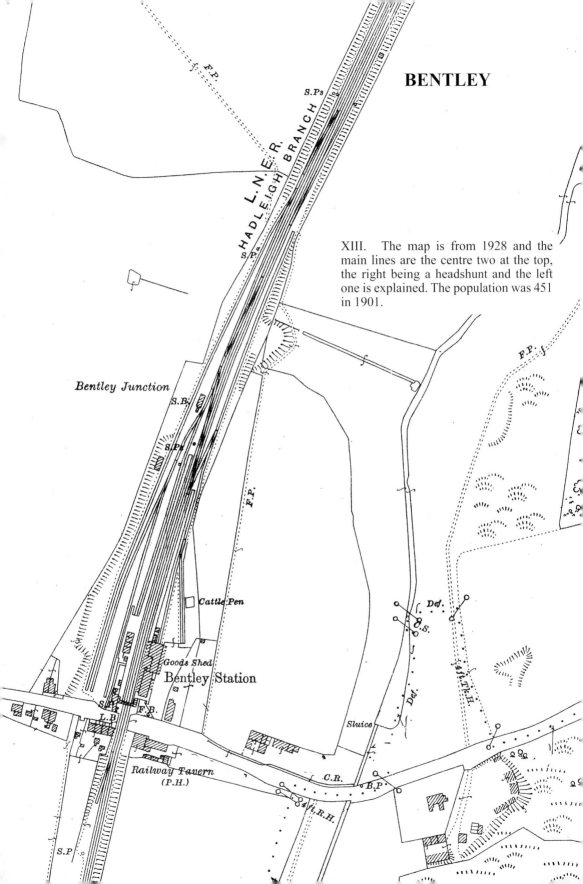

**BENTLEY**

L.N.E.R.

HADLEIGH BRANCH

S.Ps

S.P.

S.P.

XIII.   The map is from 1928 and the main lines are the centre two at the top, the right being a headshunt and the left one is explained. The population was 451 in 1901.

F.P.

F.P.

Bentley Junction

S.B.

S.P.

F.P.

Def.

O.S.

Cattle Pen

F.P.

Goods Shed

Bentley Station

Sluice

Def.

R.H.

L.B.

F.B.

S.

C.R.

B.P.

Railway Tavern
(P.H.)

R.H.

S.P.

104.    We gaze east down a quiet lane towards a stream which flows into the River Stour. The station buildings and footbridge are on the left of this tranquil scene. (P.Laming coll.)

105.    This southward view is from another postcard and the sign suggests that you can change here for the Hadleigh branch. This closed to passengers in 1932 and to freight in 1965. There was a triangular junction until the 1870s, when the northern side was lifted. (P.Laming coll.)

106.    Looking north on 30th September 1956, we note the well kept gardens. The goods yard closed on 13th July 1964 and passenger service was withdrawn on 7th November 1966. Bentley Junction signal box lasted until 30th June 1975. There was Belstead box further west until 28th April 1929. It was near the summit of notable gradients. (R.M.Casserley)

## SOUTH OF
## IPSWICH

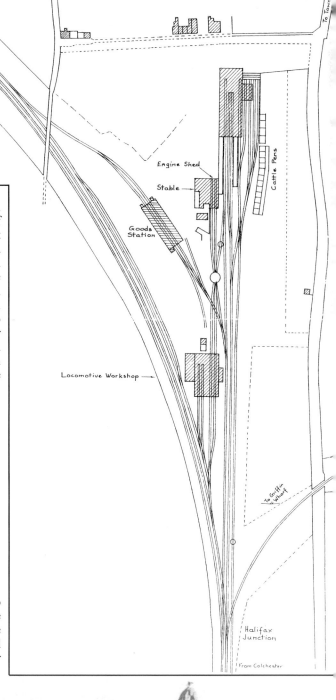

XIV.    The tunnel to the present station is top left and the branch to Griffin Wharf is on the right of this diagram from about 1850. Halifax Junction (lower) had a signal box until 23rd August 1970 and it is shown on the next map, near the word EASTERN. Trains of the Ipswich & Bury Railway first used the tunnel for goods from 30th November 1846 and for passengers from 24th December of that year. The wharf branch opened in September 1848 and was soon doubled. The EUR and the I&BR were amalgamated on 9th July 1847.

107.    Trains from Colchester ran into a terminus for many years and those running north had to reverse back. The station was south of the tunnel and this drawing is thought to show it after changes were undertaken in 1850. (BR)

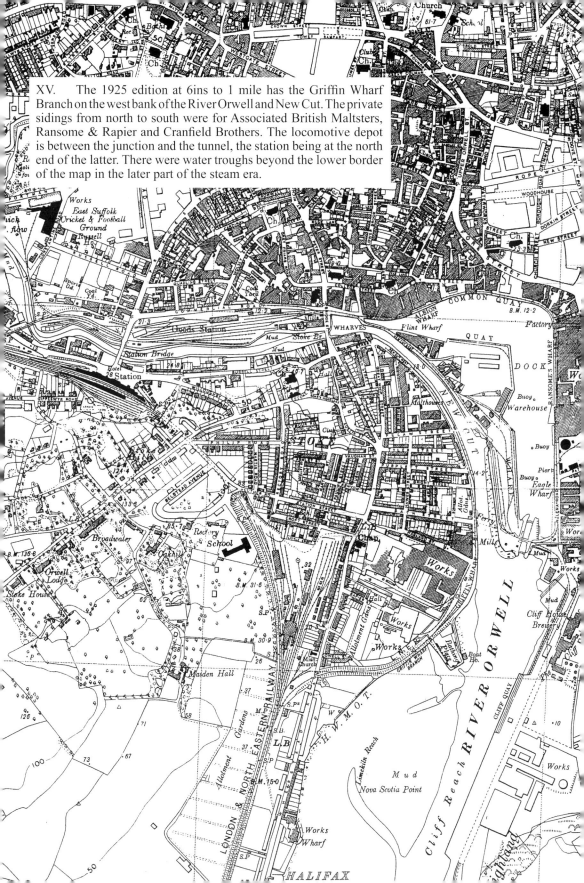

XV.    The 1925 edition at 6ins to 1 mile has the Griffin Wharf Branch on the west bank of the River Orwell and New Cut. The private sidings from north to south were for Associated British Maltsters, Ransome & Rapier and Cranfield Brothers. The locomotive depot is between the junction and the tunnel, the station being at the north end of the latter. There were water troughs beyond the lower border of the map in the later part of the steam era.

108.    The locomotive depot was developed on the site of the terminus and this view south has the engine shed and water tower in the left background, with the wagon repair shop on the right. The large coal lumps were stacked by hand and the small material was shovelled in behind. Staff facilities were crude; there was no canteen and there was just one flush for six seats; there was no roof. (NRM)

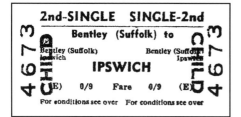

109. There had been about 90 locomotives allocated here in 1950, but this was down to 60 in 1957. Only 27 diesels were needed to take over their work in 1959. This is the scene on 16th July 1953 as work was in progress to modernise the facilities. Completion was in 1954, when the workshops on the right were repaired and the smoke chutes removed. Officially steam ended in November 1959 and operationally closure was in 1968. (BR)

110.    Recently withdrawn class 15 Bo-Bo diesels stand outside in 1971 prior to their disposal for scrapping. This is the southern part of the new roof, the northern frames being evident in the background of the previous picture. DMUs are stored on the right. The diesel depot had a four-road running shed, flanked by a two-track maintenance shop and a fitting shop on the west side. (S.Davies/D.Brennand coll.)

→    111.  We look south on 31st July 1975 from the southern portal of Ipswich Tunnel, which is 361yds in length. In the centre is the wagon works, which was created on the site by the EUR. The area was used by the electrical engineers in the 1980s and is now occupied by dwellings. (D.C.Pearce)

→    112. There was a rare opportunity to visit Griffin Wharf in brake vans on 20th January 1990 on the Branch Line Society's "Orwell Docker IV", which was hauled by no. 08775. The trip ran on to other quays. (D.C.Pearce)

# IPSWICH

113.   The station opened on 1st July 1860 and was served by electric trams from 1903 until 1926 and then by trolleybuses until 1963. The building dates from 1860 and an island platform was added in 1883. The town grew from 66,630 souls in 1901 to 119,440 in 1961. (P.Laming coll.)

➔   114.  Ipswich Goods Junction box lasted until 11th April 1984, as did Station box. This is the former. Many colour light signals had come into use in July 1957. (A.Vaughan)

➔   115.  The island platform is in the background as we look north at the carriage sidings on 12th June 1957. The locomotive top left obscures the turntable; this is shown on the left of the last map. (J.H.Meredith)

> **Other views of Ipswich can be seen in the following Middleton Press albums: *Ipswich to Saxmundham, Ipswich Tramways* and *Ipswich Trolleybuses.***

116.     We are at the north end of the island platform and the locomotive on the right is being serviced near the turntable. Class B1 no. 61000 *Springbok* has just arrived from London on 27th May 1958. (C.Nash)

← 117. A class 47 heads an up parcels train on 26th July 1975. It is seen from above the tunnel through Stoke Hill, with carriage sidings on the left. They became a diesel depot, with the fuelling point on the left. (D.C.Pearce)

↓ 118.   The north portal of the tunnel is seen from platform 2 on 20th October 1982. The bore was closed from 19th July to 5th September 2004 for alterations to lower the trackbed to allow larger containers to be accommodated. Station box had been completed in 1883. Fuel tanks are evident in the diesel depot. (J.H.Meredith)

↑　119.　No. 47571 is pulling out with the 12.17 to London on 22nd August 1984, as preliminary work for electrification is in progress. The original building remains in use today. (H.Ballantyne)

←　120.　Our final view shows that electrification of three roads of the diesel depot had taken place and we see both types of traction at rest on 17th October 1990. The vista is from platform 4. (A.C.Mott)

**MP Middleton Press**

EVOLVING THE ULTIMATE RAIL ENCYCLOPEDIA

**Easebourne Lane, Midhurst, West Sussex.**
**GU29 9AZ    Tel:01730 813169**

www.middletonpress.co.uk    email:info@middletonpress.co.uk
A-978 0 906520  B- 978 1 873793  C- 978 1 901706  D-978 1 904047  E -978 1 906008

All titles listed below were in print at time of publication - please check current availability by looking at our
website - **www.middletonpress.co.uk** or by requesting a Brochure which includes our
*LATEST* RAILWAY TITLES also our TRAMWAY, TROLLEYBUS, MILITARY and WATERWAYS series